ABCs of Empathy

Copyright © 2025 Sig Campbell Studio

All rights reserved. No portion of this book may be reproduced in any form without written permission from the publisher or author, except as permitted by U.S. copyright law.

ISBN: 979-8-218-65432-0 (Softcover)
ISBN: 979-8-218-66802-0 (Hardcover)

Illustrations by Mauro Lirussi

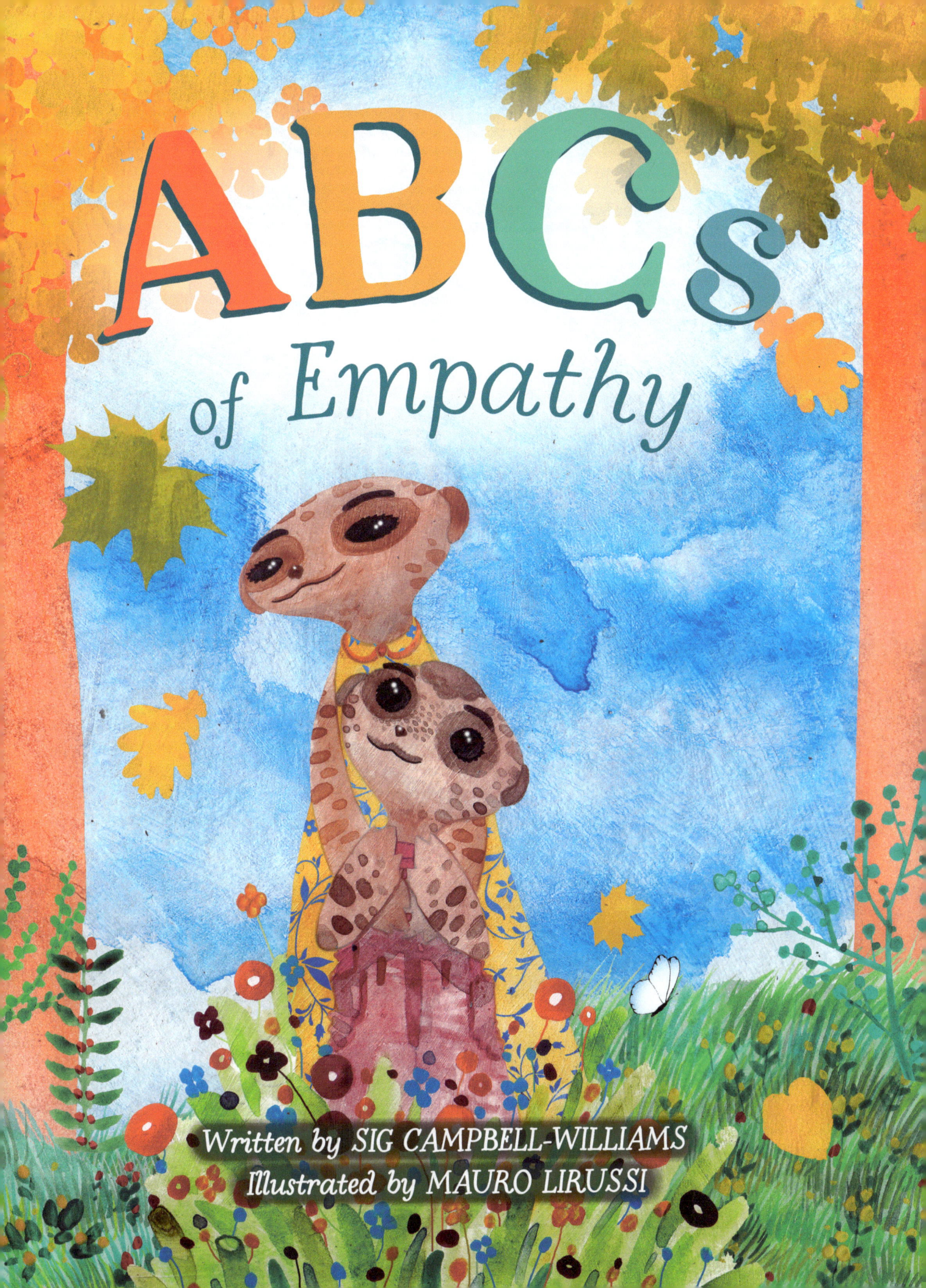

To Connor, Collin, Corbin, Everly & Berkeley - Your empathy can change the world.

A is for ATTITUDE.

It's how you feel today.
It's being mad, it's being sad,
or when you shout *hooray!*

B is for BEAUTY.

It's not so hard to see.

It's in flowers and starry nights, and people like you and me.

C is for CALM.

It's a feeling, soft and true.
It's being still in your heart
and in your mind too.

D is for DELIGHT.

It's when your heart feels bright.

It's friends sharing smiles when the feeling's just right.

E is for EMPATHY.

It's caring for how others feel.
It's knowing someone's emotions
and helping them to heal.

G is for GRACE.

It can sometimes be a name!

It's remembering your manners and treating everyone the same.

H is for HONESTY.

It means your words are true.
It can be hard to speak them,
but you'll feel better if you do.

I is for INCLUSION.

It's when each of us gets a turn.

It's hearing each others' voices, so everyone can learn.

J is for JOY.

It's feeling happy as can be.

It's like singing together
in perfect harmony.

L is for LISTENING.

It's hearing what is said to you.

It's understanding all the words,
the mind, and feelings too.

M is for MANNERS.

It's more than saying please.
It's acting kind and thankful
when no one even sees.

N is for NOBLE.

It's when you are honest and brave.

It's when you want to help others, or be the one to save.

O is for OPEN.

It's being up for something new.

It's welcoming new ideas and different points of view.

P is for PATIENCE.

It's knowing when and how to wait.

It's staying calm and staying cool,
so everyone feels great.

Q is for QUIET.

It's a hush or gentle whispers.
It's what we all should do in order to be good listeners.

R is for RESPECT.

It's when your actions show your heart.

It's looking after others as you would for yourself, directly from the start.

S is for SYMPATHY.

It's when you listen because you care. It's doing your best to understand when someone has something to share.

T is for TRUST.

It's when you believe in your family and friends.

It's knowing they'll always help you out and stick by you until the end.

U is for UNCONDITIONAL.

It's kindness without exclusion.
It's loving others no matter what,
without any confusion.

V is for VALIDATION.

It's when you're welcomed and accepted.
It's true we all are different,
and we all are connected.

W is for WISDOM.

It's all the facts we know.
It's learning from our mistakes,
so we can change and grow.

X is for XENIAL.

It's a word from Ancient Greece.
It's when you're warm and friendly,
and like keeping the peace.

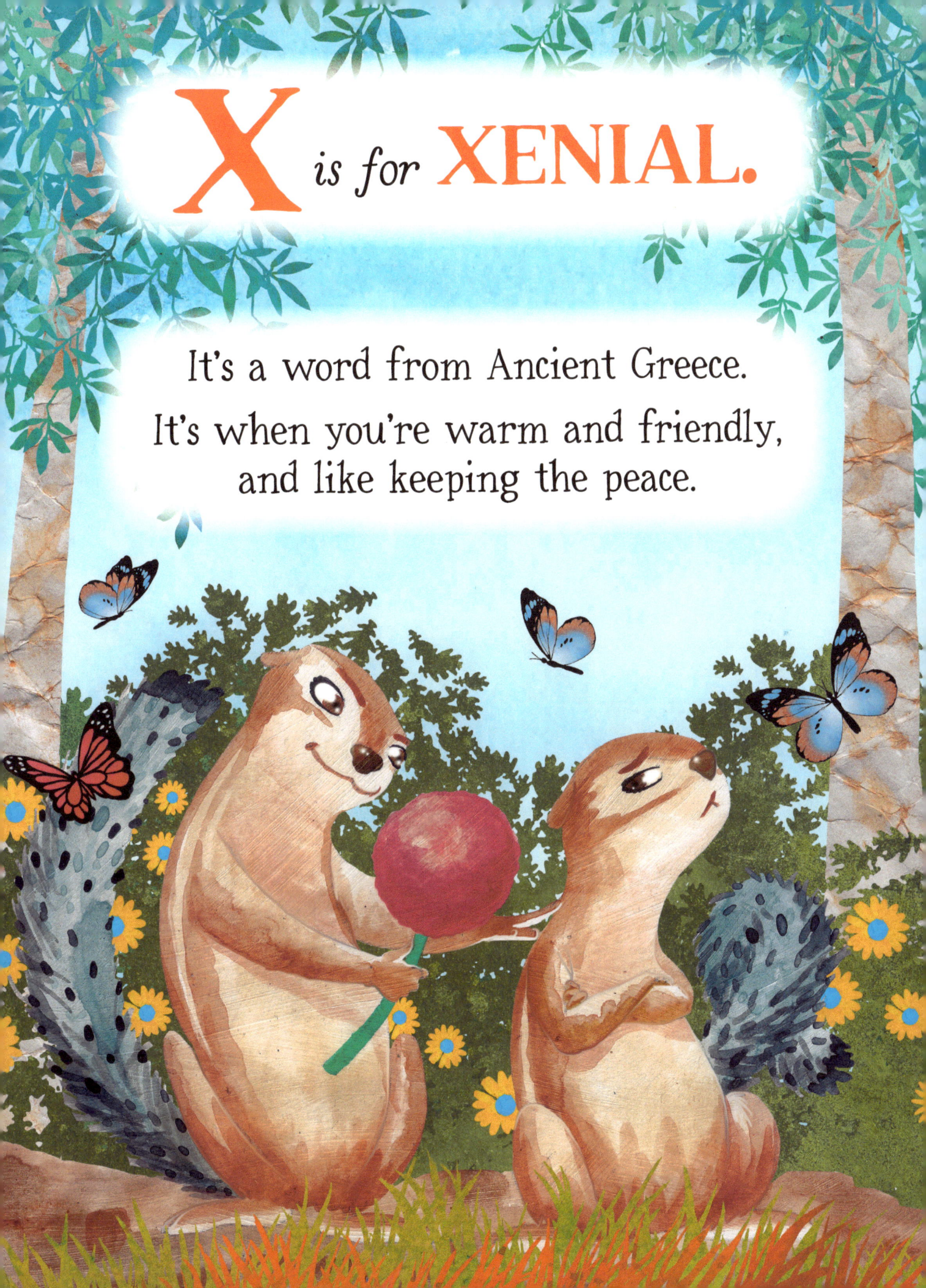

Y is for YIN AND YANG.

It's when two halves make a whole.
It's the thought there should be balance in everybody's soul.

Z is for ZEN.

It's showing calm and patience. It's giving time to yourself and others, so you'll have good relations!

www.ingramcontent.com/pod-product-compliance
Lightning Source LLC
Chambersburg PA
CBHW042056050526
44107CB00110B/1196